TOBY DOES STUFF

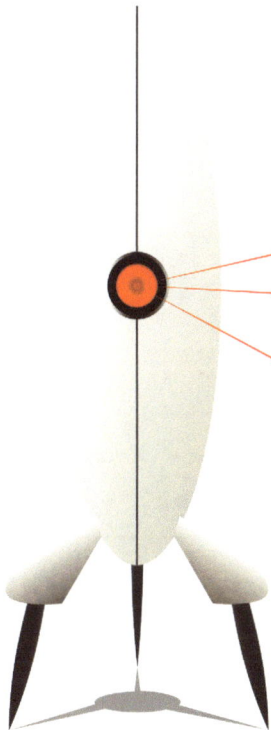

WRITTEN AND ILLUSTRATED BY
KEVIN WOLANSKI

Printed in the United States of America

First Printing: March 2016

ISBN-13 978-0-692-65501-6

DEDICATED TO

MOM
DAD
JENNA

AARON
ANDY
ALISON
BRIE
DENNIS
DEREK
FIL
JOSH
KATIE
LISA
LORI
MIKE
NICK
STEPH

THANK YOU FOR ALWAYS ENCOURAGING ME TO DO "STUFF"!

"THIS IS TOBY, HE IS A SILLY CORGI WHO IS PRONE TO DOING SILLY STUFF."

"TOBY JOURNEYS INTO THE IMAGINATION."

"TOBY AIN'T AFRAID OF NO GHOST."

"TOBY EMBARKS ON THE MOST ASTONISHING, INNOVATIVE, BACKYARD ADVENTURE OF ALL TIME."

"THAT IS NO TOBY!"

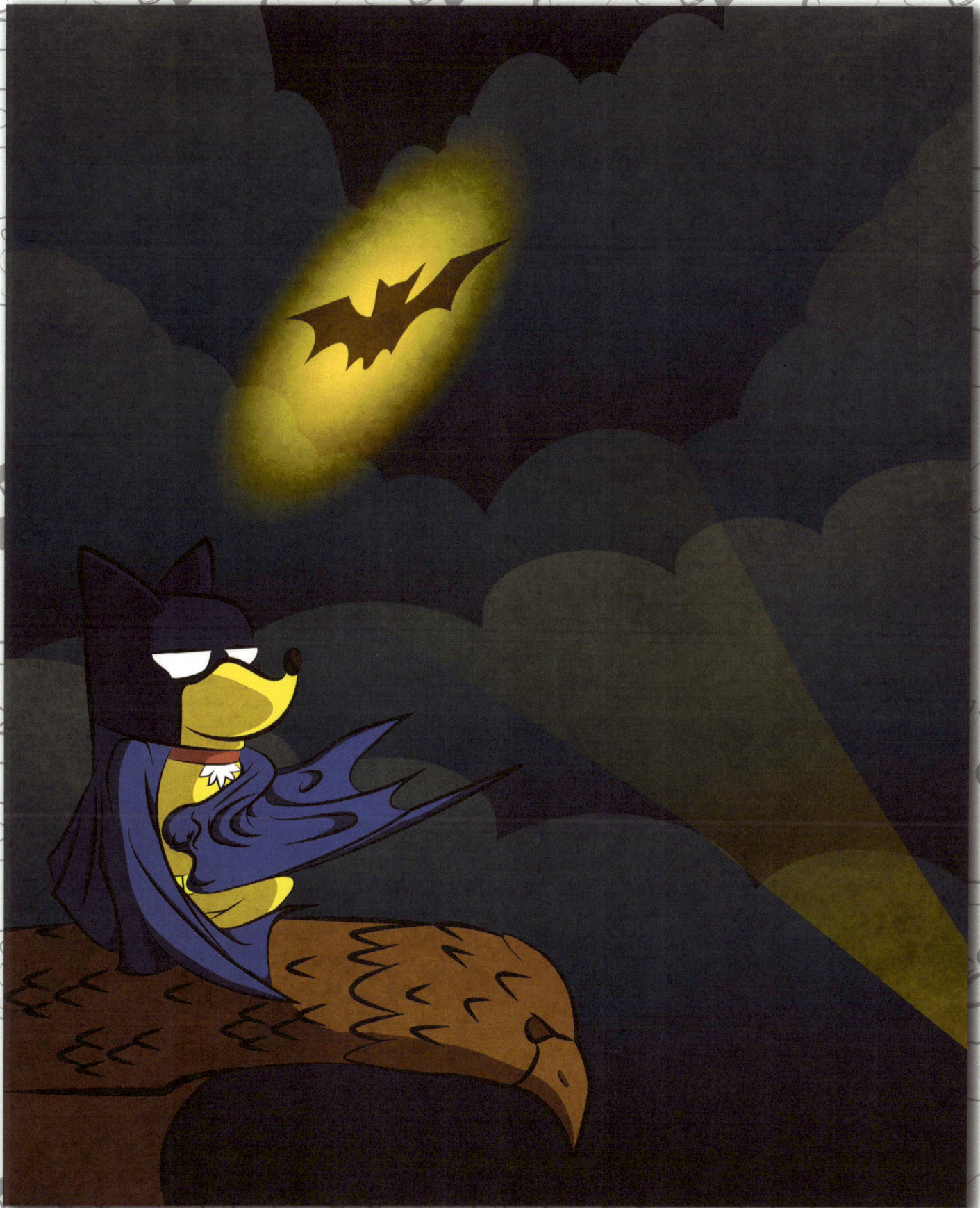

"TOBY IS THE HERO WE DESERVE."

"TOBY GOES HOME."

"WHEN TOBY HITS 88MPH YOU'RE GOING TO SEE SOME SERIOUS S#@!"

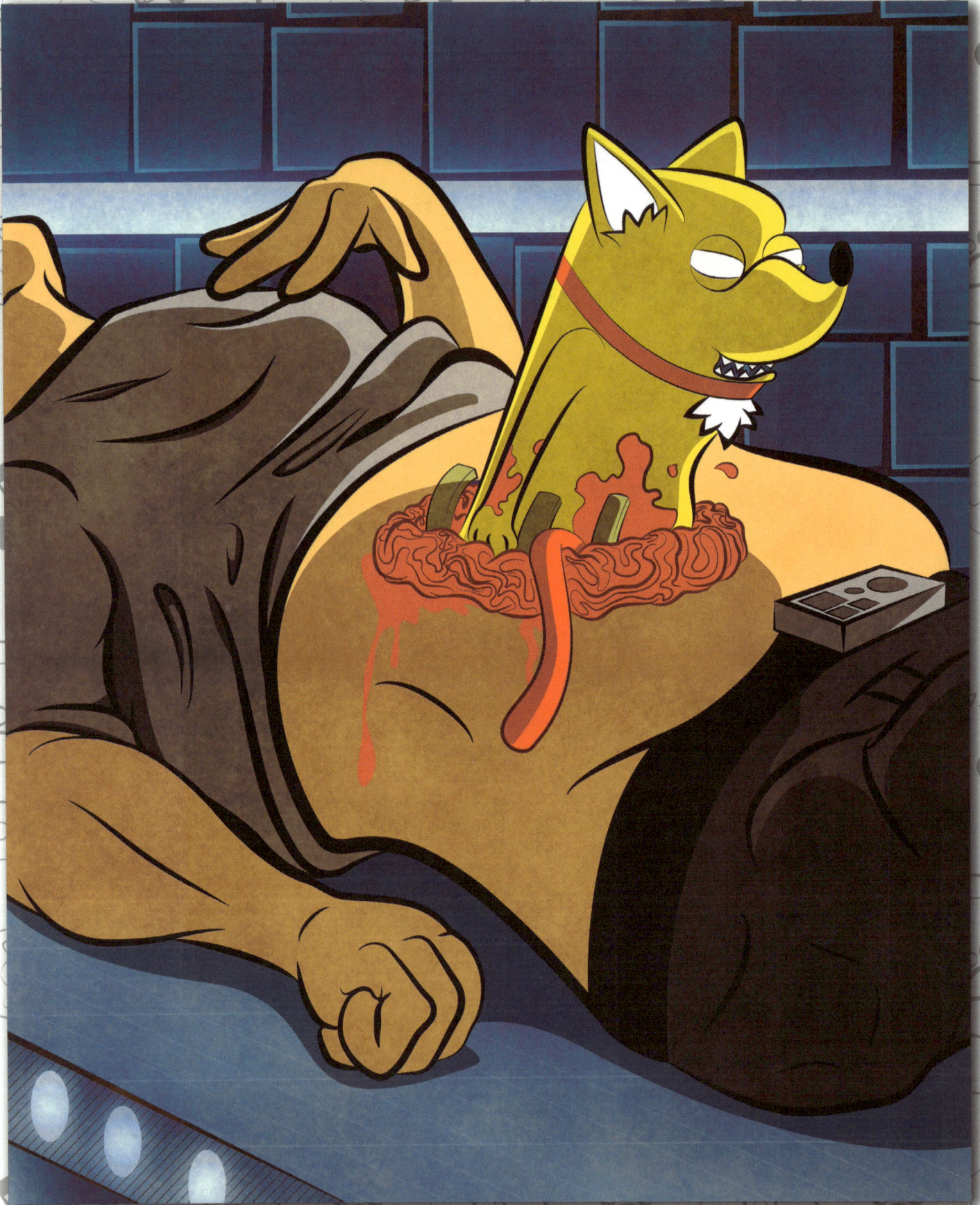

"TOBY ENJOYS SURPRISING PEOPLE."

"TOBY HAS A LICENSE TO KILL."

"TOBY IS THE FIRST AVENGER."

"TOBY'S PRINCESS IS IN ANOTHER CASTLE."

"DON'T GET HIM WET, KEEP HIM AWAY FROM BRIGHT LIGHT
AND NEVER FEED HIM AFTER MIDNIGHT."

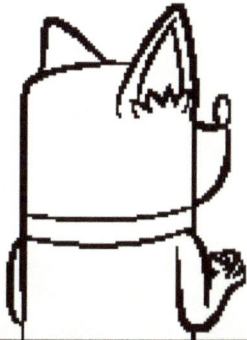

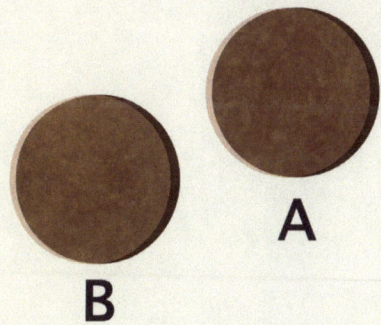

"THE WORLD IS TOBY'S."

"TOBY IMAGINES DRAGONS."

"TOBY LISTENS!"

"TOBY EMBARKS ON A SPACE ODYSSEY."

"WAKA WAKKA WAKKA WAKKA WAKKA"

"TOBY DOESN'T WANNA DO THE TRUFFLE SHUFFLE."

"TOBY KNOWS KUNG FU."

"TOBY WEARS HIS SUNGLASSES AT NIGHT."

"TOBY THINKS WITH PORTALS."

"TOBY EXPLORES A DIGITAL FRONTIER."

"TOBY WAITS FOR THE BUS."

"TOBY CAN TAKE A SUNRISE, SPRINKLE IT WITH DEW
COVER IT IN CHOCOLATE AND ADD A MIRACLE OR TWO."

"TOBY LIKES THAT OLD TIME ROCK N' ROLL."

"TOBY KNOWS WINTER IS COMING."

"TOBY IS A WIZARD."

"TOBY IS A WANDERER."

"TOBY KNOWS THIS IS THE END."

THE END

KEY

TOBY WILL RETURN

www.ingramcontent.com/pod-product-compliance
Lightning Source LLC
Chambersburg PA
CBHW041237040426
42445CB00004B/61